Grief

BY DEREK O'NEILL

ISBN: 978-1-936470-37-2
First Edition

Get a Grip Series © 2013
Editor: Nancy Moss
Front Cover Design: © 2013 by Derek O'Neill and Cléa Owens

DEDICATION

To all who read this book, I salute you for wanting to change the way you live for the better and for having the courage to be who you are as fully as possible.

To all who encourage me everyday to keep going and sharing their lives with me, family small and large. But most of all the little angels who came to teach me – Alexa and Blake, my grandchildren.

"Everybody hurts sometimes, and when we do it is nice to have Derek O'Neill around. His excellent little books on the things that get us, (fear, anger, depression, victimhood, mental blocks) allow us to find our way safely through our psychological minefields and arrive safely at the other side. Read them when you need them."

Paul Perry, Author of the
New York Times Bestseller
Evidence of the Afterlife

TABLE OF CONTENTS

AUTHOR'S PREFACE

Thank you for purchasing *Grief – Mind Boggling, But Natural*. This book has not come about as a result of my training as a therapist, but through some hard-earned lessons that I have experienced myself. This is how I know the path out of limiting beliefs and behaviors that hinder growth. The tools that I offer in this book have worked not only for me, but also for hundreds if not thousands of other people. I have shared these ideas and techniques in my workshops, one-on-one sessions, video and radio broadcasts, and on my website, and I have witnessed astounding results time and time again. Through observation of others, and myself, I have learned to identify the triggers and root causes of disharmony. Most of all, I have come to understand and apply the best methods for achieving peace and balance in life; not perfection, but real transformation and harmony that comes with learning who we are and what makes us tick. My 35 years of martial arts study has given me a refined sense of timing for when to strike with the sword to cut away old patterns, and when to use the brush to paint the picture of the life we deserve and can have.

The 'Get a Grip' series of books offers tangible, authentic wisdom that can help you in all aspects of your life. You've made a great choice by investing in this book. Enjoy the read, and take time to learn and apply the techniques. Let's change who we are together.

Derek

Grief

Mind boggling, but natural

THE TRANSIENT NATURE OF LIFE - IMPERMANENCE IS A GIFT

Grief is one of the most difficult emotions we face as humans. Loss shifts our daily lives, changes our perspective, and brings about questions that confront the very meaning of existence. The most profound grief is evoked when someone we care about dies, but grief can be a significant element of divorce, job loss, selling a home, losing a relationship, a pet dying, and more. Over the course of our existence, we will lose many people and things. Learning how to process grief with self-compassion and acceptance has a positive affect on our overall experience of life.

Grief is a natural reaction to the absence of someone or something, but understanding grief, and changing our relationship to it, is vital in the journey to lasting happiness and fulfillment. This is the gift inherent in grief. It is a reminder of how both joy and sorrow visit us, and why we must learn to "let go" with gratitude and compassion.

Once you accept that grief will visit you repeatedly, you begin to see how it is just a part of the whole. Grief is not an experience that lies outside of "the way life is supposed to be." The only "way" that life is meant to be is a mix of joy and sorrow, achievement and disappointment, enlightenment and confusion, and every other kind of ebb and flow. Our western cultures tend to build a well-fortified denial of loss – especially death – that stands in the way of productive, healing grief. To repress grief is just as dangerous as misunderstanding it and allowing it to take over our psyche. Both denying grief and becoming obsessed with it will have adverse affects on the quality of life.

Grief that originates from a major loss in our lives feels very personal. Although we know that others have experienced similar emotions, its occurrence can be isolating, no matter how much support and love those around us offer. Grief is different for everyone and each situation. It embodies its own set of changes and unfolds over varying periods. Grief speaks to the very core of who we are as individuals, but understanding the larger concept of the transient nature of all our lives is an important first step in dealing with the anguish that so often comes after loss.

Everything is impermanent, and the impermanence of everything is our great gift. That might be a difficult concept to make sense of when our culture is constantly sending us the message that "gain" is the goal, and that "loss" is something to avoid at all costs. The reality is, nothing lasts. Life is always changing. When you hold on to anything – an experience, a person, or a situation - you must be prepared to let it go. The gift of impermanence, once you accept it, is that your happiness and peace of mind are no longer dependent on what happens in your life, but rather on your mindset and the actions you take, no matter what comes your way.

Impermanence is always present, even when things seem solidly stable and secure. A friend, a family member, a husband, a wife, a pet, a house, or a job will transition, whether we see it coming or not. Your attachment to that person or thing is going to determine how you are affected by the loss. Holding on to something or someone, denying impermanence, will cause great suffering when change transpires. Change is inherent in life. It may feel like disruption and upheaval, but that reaction springs from the way we erroneously define loss and grief. Though often perceived as surprising or troubling, change is the most natural, authentic part of life. It is a measure of normal progression. Grief exists as a way to heal, grow, and inspire us to live a meaningful life.

It is not easy to lose someone or something, but if you want to learn how to process grief in a way that leaves you stronger and more evolved, you must practice the art of detachment. Detachment does not mean you are uncaring, that you go on your merry way with ease, or that you never experience grief. Detachment encompasses all of your feelings, but then lets them go – in the same way you let the person or thing that you lost leave with acceptance. You cannot hold on to what is impermanent, which is everything in your life. Your mind is all that you can control.

Death is a part of life. When you grasp any person, thing, or experience, thinking they are the definition of your life, grief will debilitate you. You have a choice. If you move through loss with grace and kindness towards yourself and others, grief can have a transformative effect. An event will cause you to suffer only if you allow it. The most difficult emotion you will undergo in this lifetime will be loss, but it is coming. We are all going to the same place. What is the use of grasping what cannot be grasped? Yes, it hurts. There is a void when you lose something or when someone dies, but that emptiness and feeling of loss can be your gift to that person to carry with them and help them onto the other side. You do that by giving them permission to go, even knowing that you will have a deep emptiness inside you. That hollowness fills again the day you realize there is no death aside from the physical, since energy lives on.

We have all heard the phrase, "I'd give anything to have them back" about a loved one who has died. You might have even expressed it yourself. When someone says that, I respond "Anything? Okay, I tell you what - you can have your cat back but I want your house, your family, and every other pet that you will ever have, and by the way, I'll take your life as well. Now do you want your cat back?" We should try to focus on cherishing the people and things that are still in our lives. Wishing to trade our losses for what we do have is an impossible scenario and a useless emotion. Similarly, feeling as if you are alone in experiencing loss and grief - or that you are being punished, or cursed - is not based in reality. You are human. You will be in constant flux during the course of your life, and you will experience losses of all kinds.

"This too shall pass" is an incredibly powerful statement. There is nothing that will be here forever. One person goes, and another person arrives. One experience or circumstance ends, another begins. We are recycled in the truest sense of the word. Just like the people and things that come in and out of our lives, emotions do also, along with the circumstances from which they arise.

Happiness and sadness are transient. They too shall pass.

LOSS AND LETTING GO

How can you prepare for the storms of life, especially when many losses and tragedies arrive suddenly? Throughout your life, there is an all-encompassing wisdom of acceptance available to you. If you truly understand that you cannot protect yourself – or anyone else – from loss and grief, and know how to tap into the wisdom of acceptance, it can help you in any situation.

You can adopt a calm approach to your life, before, during, and after the storms hit. Learn to meditate and be at peace when you are happy so it becomes a way of living. If you have practiced serenity, you will be able to meet grief and sorrow with an open and healing heart. The goal is to find the stillness and harmony that resides inside you, even in times of crisis. You must stay centered and connected, otherwise you will find yourself caught in the chaos that is going on around you. Attitude is everything.

The fear of grief is rooted in thinking that you can control life. If you accept the truth of the universe having its own plan, when loss comes you will be able to move through a process of healing and acknowledgment. You can live more abundantly, having found a new perspective that can positively affect your priorities. Otherwise, a cloud of anxiety about loss, even before it arrives, cripples you.

We have more tragedy in our heads than will ever happen to us. Negativity can have a huge impact on creating our present and future quality of life. When worry overtakes you, draw a line under it. By that, I mean, stop, look at the anxiety, and shine a positive light on it. That light will help to uncover any dark recesses of your mind. A room that has not seen any illumination for billions of years loses its whole identity when somebody strikes a match. It is also a reminder of the nature of impermanence. All it takes to eliminate darkness is opening the door to the sunshine. Draw a line under the thoughts and bring them into your consciousness. Come back to your center, and if you see you are straying into negativity, draw the line again.

Never repress an emotion. Repressed grief can fester and manifest as anger, depression, and disconnection from your authentic self. Osho, an East Indian spiritual teacher, said "if you're going to be something, be it 100%." So, if you are going to be angry, be 100% angry. If you are going to be happy, be 100% happy. Whatever you feel or do, experience it 100%. There is great wisdom in that concept. If you want to eliminate something, acknowledge it 100%, then release it 100%.

Grief is part of the continuum on a scale of emotion, with happiness and sadness on different ends of that scale. Our point of reference about happiness and sadness is always shifting, depending on what we are experiencing. If you are extremely happy now, at some stage in your life you are going to be extremely sad. Give thanks and gratitude when you are happy.

Grief comes from all sorts of drama coming into our lives - you lose your house, a loved one, a boyfriend, or a girlfriend. Loss will always send you into some form of drama - always. Think about that connection. It can even be triggered by small events. When someone says, "I don't like your makeup," that is loss – loss of face! It is loss of image and confidence. Your mind allows you to be hurt and go into grief. It is vitally important that we all learn how to use the part of the mind called the critical mind, or the critical factor. The critical factor is the part of the mind that goes into self-analysis and sorts out what is objective reality, instead of the mind trying to convince us of something.

We tend to want to know what will happen. What is going to occur with our careers, children, partners, health, and financial situation? We want to feel safe and secure about the people and things we care for. The key is to not attach to the physical presence of the people and things that populate our lives, but rather connect to the wonderment of creation even in what seems like life's darkest moments. When you experience loss, or worry, ask yourself "I wonder what's going to happen next?" It is a very powerful statement. If you want to stop your mind from going down a negative path, try it. Think about your house, your family, or anything else, then say, "I wonder what's going to happen next?" Instead of receiving a concrete answer, you will find that your consciousness opens to manifestation. That manifestation comes from the wonderment and awe of creation. The reason why we find it difficult to let things go is that a lot of us have lost the connection to the incredible power of creation.

We are beautiful organisms, constantly dying and living, constantly cycling through this life of joy and laughter, and of sorrow and fear. We often forget the wonderment of it all. We create our reality. If you lose the sense of awe when you smell a rose, you are in deep trouble. If you smell some garbage, and you lose the sense of amazement, you have the same problem. There is no difference between a rose and garbage. The rose will be gone soon, turned to garbage. That is how creation works. It is a constant cycle of creation and deconstruction, and of cause and effect.

Grief finds balance with all the other qualities of life. The range of human emotion and experience that come to us is remarkable.

Never lose your sense of awe. If you do, try to get it back. Discover what drives you. What makes you feel enthusiastic and passionate? Get up, meet life, and grab it! If you try to chase it, or hold on to it too tightly, you will find that it is slippery, like a jellyfish. In time, you realize that having that fish come to you is the way you must live. Let all experiences – even grief – arrive at your doorstep. Invite them in, knowing they will not stay forever. Nothing does. This knowledge is central to learning to let go.

KARMA, ENERGY, AND THE CONTINUUM OF TIME

Science tells us that everything is energy and that it is impossible to destroy. We also find this concept in spirituality. When you accept that each of us are just energy, you can begin to shed the fear of loss, death, and the unknown. A fuller, more satisfying life arrives from that perspective. Knowing that grief will visit you, yet not devastate every aspect of your life, will help to put loss and death in perspective. The energy of grief can go from a negative framework to a positive, transformative one over time.

We do not truly hold, own, or possess anything or anyone. You probably will not be here in 100 years! We are passing through this existence as energy. That is reality, as opposed to thinking that we, and the things around us, are real. If you believe that someone is only their physical self, and then that person disappears from your life, where does that leave you? In grief, sorrow, and sadness that will last a very long time, unresolved. The illusion that something has been taken away will persist. Nothing can vanish if you do not actually own anything. Time, and our place in it, runs on a continuum. It keeps on going, changing, and always reflecting a range of experiences, things, and people. They are all exchanging places on the continuum. One goes out, and another comes in.

Karma, based on the Sanskrit word, exists in many Eastern belief systems, including Hinduism and Buddhism. It reflects the idea that our actions, and actions in past existences, will determine our future lives. It revolves around the concept of cause and effect in relation to rebirth. It is a mistake to think that fate or destiny is written in stone. Karma embodies the potential to change and transform, according to our actions. Every moment of your life is creating your future karma.

How does grief fit into the concept of karma? Contemplating the principles of karma gives us a context for a larger picture of our existence, and lessens the suffering of grief. Whatever our belief system, we can apply a model of understanding the mutable and fluctuating nature of life to our own truth. Understanding death, instead of denying or avoiding it, prepares and informs us.

If we look at life through a karmic lens, our importance becomes – ironically - both diminished and heightened. Our existence is relatively short in the present physical body we inhabit, even if we live to an old age. At the same time, we are connected to a life force, and a continuum of time, that is bigger and deeper than any individual earthly presence. When someone dies, there is emptiness and a loss, but if you look beyond suffering, you will see that emptiness and loss can be your gift to that being, something they carry with them to help them onto the other side and transform to another existence. You give them permission to go, even knowing that you will experience a vacuum. That void fills the day that you realize that there is no death, as we typically define it.

Death is an illusion. Your physical form is going to constantly change. Your journey – and all that it entails, including grief and loss – is given to you. You do not go down a spiritual path to have a happy life. You travel on it to stir up all the garbage, and look at it, so it does not follow you from one existence to another. You can sit at the bar for two hundred lifetimes but eventually you have to get off the stool! That is why you are here. Once you start digging deeper, something begins to shift in you that outweighs your fears and strengthens your resilience to grief.

How do we get to that point where we understand that death is an illusion and as simple as changing your clothes? Do departed loved ones come back and tell you? Actually, sometimes they do. Alternatively, it could be other people – right in front of you – showing you the inherently continuous nature of life, but you may not hear or see them. Grief walks in the door with happiness, and happiness walks in the door with grief. You have to embrace both.

Repeatedly, the question arises, "Why do bad things happen to good people?" When a kind, generous, humble person is taken off the planet, while someone who is creating pain, or destruction, or violence, lives on, we wonder if there is any justice to life. The death of a young person seems "unnatural." You have to surrender to the truth that the length of our time here is arbitrary. In order to survive you cannot sink into an attitude that "life isn't fair." Expanding your concept of our existence, as mutable, timeless, and enduring, is the way to be "fair" to yourself and to those who pass in this life. Grief can be an expression of that transition if we allow it to enlighten us. Knowing that death is not the final destination helps us to process grief.

You can say that we are here out of ignorance if, in a past life, we forgot our truth and acted in a way that caused suffering to others and ourselves. Now that we are more discerning, our awareness has grown. We are more conscious of our actions because we have been graced with insight, teachings, self-examination, and an understanding of existence. Your present actions are not only reliving your past karma, they are creating your new karma. Always keep in mind that karma just means movement.

GRIEF AS A PATH TO ENLIGHTENMENT

It takes both positive and negative forces to create light. Life is the dynamic of a struggle between contending dynamics. If we think we can have peace and harmony all the time, we will be disappointed. This is what the Buddha taught. The quest for unshakable happiness leads only to sadness when that happiness proves to be transient. Trust in happiness and serenity arriving again, and leaving again. If you confront grief from that perspective and learn from it, you can move forward in your life with new awareness and understanding.

We are attracted to pleasure and averted by pain. Looking at that exchange of energy, and comprehending how pain is pleasure's twin, is part of our journey to enlightenment and a more satisfying life. Without pain, you would not be here. Every birth comes with pain for someone. Creation shares this world with disruption. When there is disturbance and strife going on in the planet, the door opens for renewal. Humanity is receiving a chance to love itself again.

When someone we love dies, or we suffer another major loss, the grief can be overwhelming and potentially destructive, yet we can learn to move through it with awareness and self-compassion. The normal feelings of shock and sadness can spiral into deep dysfunction and depression. There is often guilt and anger associated with grief, and a host of other psychological and physical manifestations. At first we might feel numb before the reality of the loss sets in. Eventually there is acknowledgment and healing.

How do we get to the recovery? How do you find, ultimately, a positive result in the form of deeper insight and humanity, and experience grief productively? Accepting your loss is a difficult, but necessary first step. You cannot fully experience grief, as a constructive emotion, unless you do. When you process that grief in whatever time frame you need, you can then adjust to – and honor - the loss in your life, and devote your energies to everything else that matters around you.

Moving beyond desire or delusion is challenging yet possible by using teachings and an understanding of the power of our thoughts and attitudes as tools to "let go" and surrender to loss. Death seems especially insurmountable and unfathomable. Though not as final or heightened as death, the loss of jobs, houses, and relationships can affect you tremendously. Ultimately, we must not deny that death and loss are things we will have to face with the same source of wisdom and mindfulness that we approach other aspects of suffering in our lives. Grief comes to inform us and enlighten us. It is painful, but provides the perspective and appreciation for joy.

Facing death helps to give life its meaning. The role of faith – however you define it - is a powerful resource in process of recovery. No matter what your religious affiliation or participation, the most important aspect of spirituality is the connection to ourselves and others. To quote the cliché, "we are spiritual beings having a human experience."

TRANSITION AND TRANSFORMATION – CHANGE IS ALWAYS CHANGING

When someone dies, his or her journey here is finished. For friends and family, teachings and wisdom about impermanence and acceptance can be a source of comfort. Death is not an unknown. It is certain that death will come, one way or another, and on its own time schedule. As a person's physical form leaves us, they cannot take any of the "things" they acquired in this life, which are meaningless in the big picture. The gift they are able to carry with them to their next existence is your strength, clear state of mind, and the permission you give them to let go. You allow them to experience what is the most profound manifestation of transition and transformation that we know of in this life.

Grief itself will change over time, in ways we cannot predict from the outset. The feeling of "life will never be the same," is valid in every possible way we can define that statement. Life has changed, tremendously, but it will keep on changing – for the better, for the worse, and then back and forth again.

The stages of grief follow a general pattern. There are different models, including a three-step process - shock, sadness, acceptance, and the well-known "five stages of grief" - denial, anger, bargaining, depression, and acceptance. Each of us will have our own particular journey on a universal path. Everyone goes down it, as all of our surviving loved ones will when we die. We can gain strength and suggestions for coping with it from others, along with important support, but our grief takes its own course. The conscious decision to recognize grief, invite it in, and then release it, is the framework of how we can influence it, yet grief can always surprise you. There may be periods when your focus will shift away from the loss, then times, perhaps many years later, when a life event or circumstance will call up grief again.

Grief has many faces, from the stabbing pain of recent loss, to the long-term shift in perspective. It can inform our choices about how we live, and change our priorities and motivations. Grief may numb us initially, but in time can cause us to feel more deeply, helping us to have a conscious connection to the loved one who has passed from this existence, or to help others through their losses. Instead of the emptiness that grief highlights after a loss, grief can build a bridge to a mindfulness that encompasses something much larger than just this mortal life.

Loss and death humbles us. It defeats the arrogant and misguided idea that we can control things around us. Death offers the opportunity for gratitude and wider perspective toward all the wonders and mysteries of life and beyond. If there were no death, we would lose the context of who we are as beings on this earth. Though we may go through periods of fear or denial about death, it exists, sometimes quietly, in every aspect of how we live. It creates humanity. Life springs from death and loss.

GRIEF, COMPASSION, AND SERVICE

Whether the loss is personal, or has happened to someone we know, or affects our global community, compassion and service become positive, life affirming elements of grief. Grief can be the inspiration behind reaching out, either in our meditations and prayers, or with supportive action. Lighting a candle is a symbol for remembrance and a guide for the departed on their journey from this existence. It quite literally illuminates our human compassion and love. When we hear of accidents, natural disasters, or acts of violence, grief connects us and evokes empathy. Even if not directly affected by the loss, we know, because we are human, that the people left behind will begin a journey.

If a tragic loss occurs, there is shock and deep sadness, especially when someone young dies. We tend to want some semblance of order to life and death, and often hang on to the idea that a person needs to complete their life in order for it to make sense for them to pass on. In reality, a young life lost is just as complete as an older person's death. Whatever stretch of time we have in this existence is exactly as long as we are supposed to be here. It is the quality - not the quantity - of our existence that matters. Even a baby leaves a mark on the continuum of time. As painful as it is, we have to let go of the idea that there is some kind of injustice in loss that seems tragic. We must integrate the concept that no one is immune from death and the transient nature of life.

There is power in prayer and meditation that can directly help the souls that pass on, and their loved ones. It is our service to one another to manifest this compassion. We should always be sending out the conscious energy of sympathy and holding it mindfully for the world. An incredibly strong meditation is to say, "There is no tragedy that can shake me from my belief that all is well," even if the adversity seems overwhelming. When you start to look beyond yourself and help others, whether it's with service, charitable monies, or even just with your consciousness, you are turning grief into giving. When souls are leaving the planet and you have the ability to sit still and meditate on compassion, they can utilize your energy to cross over without fear.

The manifestation of enduring happiness for yourself – the kind that accepts that there will be times of sadness and grief - will only come when you serve another being. It is very rewarding knowing someone who is suffering or in pain feels relief because of what you said or did. Money, possessions, or status, will never trump that energy. Service IS your path to what is rightfully yours. Service will bring you joy. Helping others is a beneficial, positive expression of grief when dealing with loss. It is easy to have empathy for somebody who is suffering – you do not need to have absolute enlightenment, or be a healer. People heal themselves all the time. You are an important witness to their healing when you hold loving compassion for them.

Loss and death are the ultimate acts of surrender and devotion to the continuum of time and its divine nature. We are here to learn to give, and to receive, and the process of mourning loss and death is a perfect reflection of that. Your life derives meaning from how you choose to approach the journey and give of yourself. We receive a finality of our earthly presence to remind us that we are the same – we all die and bring only our spirit to another existence. Each of us deserves the same love, kindness, and compassion as any other being. In the end, our ultimate service is to give ourselves away. If we look at the loss of a loved one from that perspective, we remember that there are larger forces at work. That person has finished their time here and is needed elsewhere.

GRIEF AND MINDFULNESS

When we grieve, an important process of acceptance and renewal begins. If we do not have an outlet for sorrow, emotions internalize and develop into anger, depression, and a disconnection from feeling. There are many manifestations of grieving, some healthy, healing, and unselfish; others focused on self-pity, fear, or narcissistic motivations. Being mindful of how we grieve is the goal, rather than feeling as if there is only one way to move through loss and death. Even though life has undoubtedly shifted, remaining aware of the workings of your consciousness and the choices you make during difficult times, helps you in every challenge you encounter. No matter if you are going through good times or bad, bringing your consciousness back to the neutral place in-between keeps you prepared and strong for the pendulum of life's experiences.

If you can find harmony and comfort in the impermanence we all face, you will live a peaceful life. That does not mean there will not be difficult situations and occurrences. When something we thought was constant and unshakable changes, and we are shocked and devastated, sometimes questioning the belief system we held leading up to the shift would be helpful. It is a mistake to think that things will not happen that we don't want to happen! Impermanence may seem harsh, but it is an embodiment of the beautiful nature of our existence. You must make transience your friend. Be mindful of your sadness and grief. Missing someone or something is part of the process, but how you carry on is just as important, to both yourself, and in the case of a death, to the person who has left this world.

Grief after a death highlights the loss of not just a person or thing, but also the definitions we have of ourselves. Wife, mother, husband, brother, sister, child – these are the dynamics of who we are in relation to the loved one. When they are gone, we quite naturally think about our identity moving forward. Grief that is part of a healing process brings us back to the idea that we exist independent of external labels, circumstances, and indicators. We are our consciousness and our mindfulness. You will always be your parent's child, or your siblings' brother/sister, etc., death doesn't take that away. Instead, it shines a light on reconnecting with who we are at our core, and that our lives are ALWAYS going through change. We are the laughter, tears, joy, and mourning. We are our journey through the ebb and flow of life.

Grief leaves us with memories. This is our gift, to keep them alive, yet accepting that a door has closed, and there will be no more memories to come, whether because of death, divorce, the end of a relationship or any other shift, is extremely difficult. The finality stops the earthly story, but there is a spiritual story that is always being written. It's impossible to live in the past. In the case of death, we have to find a way to bring the incarnation of that person's existence into our lives, in whatever form motivates us and inspires us. What would they want for you? How can you celebrate them? What can you do to help in the world, in their spirit? What path to healing would they wish for you?

Just as we cannot live in the past, the future is not here yet. You only know this very moment. It is all you can count on, along with the nature of your consciousness. If you adopt a mindful approach to the ever-changing circumstances in which we live – and die – you have made peace with reality. Anything else – denial, desire, avoidance, and resistance – goes against the stream of life. You cannot fight it and swim upstream.

Events will unfold in a way that have nothing to do with your control or your will. When you give up the fear and denial of loss and death, the rest of your life takes on a bold new perspective. You make peace with the idea that things are never permanent, and that this existence will end on its own schedule. You also give up expending the wasted energy trying to control what happens to you – and others - in the additional parts of your life.

Mindfulness is about focusing on the present moment. If we integrate its practice into our daily lives, we are better equipped to face grief and a healing process. Losing someone or something big can catapult us back and forth from the past, where we have our memories, to the future, where we grapple with the absence of that being or situation. Having a mindful anchor - that centers you - can provide a structure to help stand upon.

Loss and death can very easily throw us out of balance, and open up the floodgates of questions about the meaning of life and impermanence. Going through the stages of grief, with the tools of awareness and mindful observation, will help you fully feel, accept, and move forward when there is loss. When we are mindful we allow every sensation and emotion to move through us, in whatever way they need to manifest. Insight and enlightenment may take longer than you would wish. It is important to be in the moment. Grief can be excruciating but you must go down its path, one day at a time.

Our relationships with people are about connection, compassion, and love. Grief is the natural price we pay for these emotions that both enrich our lives and trigger pain when we lose a relationship or someone dies. Mindfulness brings us to the present, where we can evoke that love and connection in a new form after a person moves out of our life or passes to another existence.

ACCEPTING LOSS, ACCEPTING GRIEF

Loss and death visits all of us. Grief comes, and then goes, only to arrive again. If we continue to treat grief as something to avoid we are not only fooling ourselves, but also hurting ourselves. If there is no acceptance, there is no healing. You cannot control how loss shows up. In our experience of death, we can wish for only peaceful endings of long lives within the circle of people we care about, but there is no immunity from sudden and traumatic events. Accepting this truth at times of happiness is even more valuable than realizing it when there is a loss.

Death is the most difficult loss to accept. Different cultures have practices and rituals. Seeing the body after death is a common tool to help the mind - that can often go into denial to self-protect from pain – and acknowledge the reality of the loss. Ceremonies, sacraments, and rites serve an important purpose for both individuals and communities, but even with available outlets, accepting loss and death within your own conscious mind is an internal process. Teachings and wisdom provide the framework upon which you build your own house of healing.

Grief and gratitude are not usually thought of together, but they walk together. The insight that grief ultimately delivers is the gratitude for the time we have with the people we care about, and the gratitude we can develop about the nature of life. That nature is good and bad, joyous and sad, birth and death. Without the darkness, there is no light. We would not know we were in illumination if it did not leave us at times.

There's no replacing someone who has left us through death, but the idea that someone has become your "reason to live," is going to destroy you. It is especially hard in the case of losing a child or a spouse. The key is to shift your perspective while these people are here with you. Love can be deeper than the ocean but it is not about needing someone to be alive. We each have our story in this existence. We cannot grasp on to a different reality from the one that is meant to be, or cling to someone who is transitioning from this life. Feeling like you can't go on is not unusual but like everything else, it will change.

We hear stories about people, throughout history, who have lost everyone and everything, yet they find a way to emerge from unfathomable grief. Though most of us will never know this exact experience, we need to be in communion with everyone's losses. There are no "lucky people" vs. "unlucky people." Life and its varied, transient, non-selective nature is the source of events that happen to people – good, bad, peaceful, and traumatic.

You are fighting the natural order of life if you deny loss and try to avoid pain. Out of fear, there are individuals who run away from loss and death, sometimes abandoning people in need of emotional support, occasionally even a person who is dying. We have to be mindful not just of our own journey, but of those around us, and the actual people facing the end or a major shift. Our inability to process grief can come out in a negative way that hurts other people. It is hard for many people to even think about major loss or death, but until you integrate it into your life, you will lack the tools to take care of yourself and others who need your support during the stages of grief.

SUGGESTIONS TO HELP THE GRIEVING PROCESS

There is no easy way to go through grief. When there is a loss of any kind that disrupts our lives, the effect can be debilitating. Taking action to begin to heal and renew is often difficult when we may very well feel numb, depressed, and helpless.

When someone dies, or we divorce, or have a career shake-up, there are so many details and tasks to complete that we may ignore or avoid our emotions. There is no "correct" way to process grief, but neglecting yourself, whether it's from deep despair or putting on a brave face, is always going to make the journey harder and potentially damaging. You must find a way to take care of yourself with compassion and patience.

There's no one-size-fits-all answer for managing and moving though grief but these suggestions can make a huge difference, not just during the experience of dealing with our losses, but in how we continue to live after there is healing.

- Practice self-care: Grief takes a toll on your well-being. Though diet and exercise may be the last thing on your mind when you are going through drastic change, it is very important that you take care of yourself. Grief and trauma depletes your physical reserve. Eating healthy foods, exercising, and trying your best to sleep adequately is going to give you the energy you need. Those good practices also assist in strengthening your mind, which can feel very drained and stressed.

- Get the help you need: Seek the support of friends and family, and reach out to professionals if

you are having a difficult time.
Therapists and other mental health
care practitioners - especially those
trained in loss or bereavement - can
provide an objective, informed,
and highly personalized approach.
Do not forgo help when you feel
overwhelmed and unable to cope.
There is always someone to talk to
and assist with your healing.

- Tap into your belief systems: Turn
to the teachings, spirituality or any
other wisdom you follow, to anchor
your feelings. Connect with the
community you practice with or
belong to, for comfort, connection,
and love. Accept that we can explore
the meaning of loss and death, yet
there is so much about life that is
unknown. You have to hand over
the idea of control. Having answers
to the big questions is not our
purpose. Rather it's finding peace

and joy in the ability to think, feel, communicate, and dream.

- Recognize your emotions: Grief comes in nearly all shapes and sizes of emotions – shock, sadness, denial, anger, fear, guilt, hopelessness, and so on. As much as we would like to not feel these things, we do. Experience them fully. You cannot process grief, nor take in any teaching, healing direction, therapeutic help, or affirming philosophy if you do not first recognize your feelings. You have to greet your emotions, invite them in, and then begin the journey of letting them back out the door. You may very well meet the dark feelings again, in relation to your grief, but they won't have moved in to your consciousness as permanent residents.

- Keep coming back to the concept of impermanence: If we adopt a perspective that everything is changing and nothing lasts, we can weather the storms of loss and grief with a better framework. Grasping at what cannot be grasped only burdens our consciousness with an impossible wish to avoid and deny loss. As humans, we form strong attachments. It is natural that we feel loss so deeply. That is our pendulum, reflected in the constantly shifting and varying nature of life.

• Remember that grief will change: At the outset of a loss, it is hard to imagine the pain lessening and life going on, perhaps even improving. Be in the moment but see beyond your dark perspective. Grief is unpredictable. If not processed, it could be very harmful long term, but if you deal with it, even in small steps, time will start giving you the ability to heal. Though grief can pop up again suddenly, sometimes triggered years after a loss, if you have the tools of self-compassion and awareness, you can work through it again.

- Give yourself the time you need to heal: There is no schedule for how and when you move through grief. Circumstances and people are different. Loss is extremely complicated. Practice kindness and patience towards yourself. Don't let it bother you if someone says it's time you "got over it" after a certain period of time has gone by. That "advice" doesn't take into account anything relevant for you. You can feel what you feel, whenever you do. Don't force yourself to do anything before you are ready.

- Have outlets for your grief: Along with addressing grief directly, through people close to you or support groups, devote energy to creative expression, hobbies, and activities. Turn to your yoga and/or meditation practice, and if you don't have one, explore the possibilities.

- Serve others: When you help people, you heal. Grief can be a very insular and internal experience. Looking outside of yourself can shift emotional burdens and pain. We can feel very alone in our grief. Connect with your humanity. Reach out in the spirit of someone you lost. The joy and value of helping other people comes back to you, magnified, just when you need it most.

GRIEF MEDITATION

Grief manifests and progresses in ways that are unique to each individual, but all of us can benefit from meditation and mindful contemplation as part of the healing process. Remember, there is no exact prescription or time limit to processing grief. You may go through shock, denial, fear, anxiety, despair, sadness, and even disorientation. As you move through grief you will take small steps toward recovery that involve reorganizing yourself and your life. Meditation can help to center your mind and body by focusing on the self-care that is necessary to achieve that goal. Here is an example of a meditation to use when dealing with the death of someone close to you.

Take three deep breaths. Close your eyes and relax. Concentrate on each part of your body, starting with your feet and moving upward, consciously releasing tension and stress. Be mindful of your breath and as you continue to inhale and exhale. Let the heaviness of your emotions flow out of you, down through your feet and into the earth, replaced by openness and clarity.

Imagine your loved one standing in front of you right now, radiating with golden light. Feel the connection between you. Continue to breathe deeply and be mindful of how your body feels. Consciously tap into the energy uniting you and your loved one. If you can, imagine talking to them. Tell them things you might not have had a chance to say while they were here, or talk as if you would have while they were alive. As feelings arise, continue to be aware of your breath and your body. Concentrate on the light and envelop your emotions in its warmth. Allow your thoughts to flow but try to bring them back to a place of relaxation and peace. Spend time in that environment with the person who has passed, then let them go into the light. Know that you can connect with them again through memory, through the way you live your life, and through these special meditative routes.

Whether grief has arisen from death, or other types of loss, such as divorce, a relationship breakup, or a job, it is natural and normal. By looking at the positive outcomes of growth and healing that may emerge from these events, you will begin to rebuild and mend from the trauma much more easily. Seek out other meditations and stress-relieving exercises. Take as much time as you need to work with them. You will be amazed at how helpful focusing your mind and thoughts can be for your well-being.

Above all else, be kind and compassionate to your psyche and reach out for help. The fragility you feel after loss is real, but the potential for healing and renewal is even stronger. You don't have to go it alone when you are dealing with grief. There are numerous resources for professional counseling and support groups. At the very least, talk to the people you are closest to. Though some may assume that speaking about grief and your loss can bring up more pain, the opposite is true. The more you talk about your departed loved ones or other kinds of loss, and vent your feelings, the sooner you recover from grief.

ABOUT THE AUTHOR

For more than 15 years, Derek O'Neill has been transforming the lives of thousands of people around the world for the better. An internationally acclaimed transformational coach and therapist, motivational speaker, author, martial arts sensei and humanitarian, Derek inspires and uplifts people from all walks of life through his workshops, consultations, speaking engagements, media, and tireless humanitarian work.

Drawing on thirty years of training in martial arts, which earned him the level of Master Black Belt, coupled with his extraordinary intuitive abilities and expertise as a psychotherapist, Derek has pioneered a new psychology, transformational therapy. His signature process, aptly named "The Sword and the Brush," helps clients to seamlessly transmute their struggles into positive outcomes, using the sword to cut away old patterns and the brush to help paint the picture of the new life that they require.

In addition to reaching large audiences through workshops and media, Derek advises individuals, celebrities, business leaders, and politicians, helping them to find new perspectives on long-standing issues and bringing harmony back to their lives and businesses. Inspired by his worldly travels, he formed SQ Foundation, a not-for-profit organization focused on helping to solve global issues facing humanity today. In 2012, he was honored as Humanitarian of the Year and named International Celebrity Ambassador for Variety International the Children's Charity. He was welcomed as Vice President of the esteemed charity in May 2013.

Author of More Truth Will Set You Free, the Get a Grip series of pocket books, a cutting edge book on parenting titled Calm Mama, Happy Baby, and several children's books, Derek also hosted his own radio show, "The Way With Derek O'Neill," which enjoyed the most successful launch in VoiceAmerica's history, quickly garnering 100,000 listeners.

Derek is a master at offering practical wisdom and proven techniques for living a more harmonious and fulfilling life, bringing CEOs to the level of wise yogi and wise yogis to CEO; he has worked with executives from some of the world's major airlines, and the cast of Spiderman on Broadway to help transform group disharmony and untapped creative potential into productivity and dynamic performance. He has been featured in Exceptional People Magazine, The Irish Independent, The Irish Examiner, CBS television, and RTE, Ireland's national TV network.

Recordings of Derek's discourses are available for download, offering practical wisdom and proven techniques for living a more harmonious and fulfilling life.

To learn more about Derek O'Neill, to attend his next workshops, to order books, downloads, video streaming, or to contact him, please visit his website:

www.derekoneill.com

To learn more about Derek's SQ Foundation, the global charity that is changing the lives of hundreds of thousands of people around the world, go to:

www.sq-foundation.org

MORE RESOURCES FROM DEREK O'NEILL

Videos, Audio Downloads, Live Broadcasts, Books, Blog and more at **derekoneill.com**

Books
Calm Mama, Happy Baby

"Get a Grip" Book Series
Happiness - You Must Be Effin' Joking!
Anger – Who Gives a Shite?
Relationships – Would You Want to Date You?
Depression – What's that?
Weight – What's Eating You?
Confidence – Easy for You to Say
Abundance – Starts Right Now
Fear - A Powerful Illusion
Addiction - What a Cover-Up!
Excellence - You Never Lost It, You Forgot It
Grief - Mind Boggling, but Natural

Children's Books

Water Drop Coloring Book

The Adventures of Lucinda in Love-Filled
Fairyland

SOCIAL MEDIA

Follow on YouTube
www.youtube.com/user/DerekONeill101

Like on Facebook
www.facebook.com/derekoneill101

Follow on Twitter
www.twitter.com/DerekONeill101

Connect on LinkedIn
www.linkedin.com/in/derekoneill101